PALESTR

TEN FOUR-PART MOTETS
FOR THE CHURCH'S YEAR

Edited and Translated by

ALEC HARMAN

OXFORD UNIVERSITY PRESS
MUSIC DEPARTMENT 37 DOVER STREET LONDON W1X 4AH

CONTENTS

PREFACE

THE MAIN PURPOSE of this selection from Palestrina's four-part motets is to provide choir-masters with a representative work by this great Renaissance composer for the principal feasts of the church. Compared with his considerable output very little of Palestrina's music is available in modern editions that are accurate, cheap, and intended for practical use; this, considering the esteem in which he has always been justifiably held, is surprising. If this small collection whets the appetite for more and encourages choirs to explore further, then it will have fulfilled its second purpose.

My source for these motets is the Vatican edition published by Edizione Fratelli Scalera, Rome. All dynamic and speed indications, bar-lines, and small accidentals are mine. Where the text was missing in the original it is shown by square brackets; owing to the haphazard approach to underlay of Renaissance editions, the underlay in the present collection is inevitably largely editorial.

The translations of the texts have aimed firstly, at providing the same syllabic and rhythmic patterns as the Latin, and secondly, at the identical placing of those words whose meaning is reflected to some extent in a musical phrase, e.g. the opening of *Ad Te levavi*, where 'levavi' has clearly dictated the upward leaping fifth and fourth. In this connexion I must record my thanks to Jacqueline Froom for her many felicitous suggestions. My thanks are also due to the Rev. W. M. Atkins for providing the footnote to *Tribus miraculis*.

I have added very few indications of speed and expression, as changes in the former should only occur sectionally, and the latter should be governed at a general level by the meaning of the words, and individually by the fluctuating importance of each part in a polyphonic texture, and the melodic rise and fall. It is most important that the singers should appreciate the rhythmic structure of their own parts and that of all the parts together, and should realise that the bar-lines are primarily inserted as a help to ensemble, and do not imply regular accents. The rhythmic shape of each part is determined by the placing of accented notes, and these are governed by the natural stresses of the words or, where there are several notes to a syllable, by the height and length of a note relative to those adjacent to it. In order to clarify the rhythm I have added stress marks ($>$); if placed over a crotchet this mark implies that the preceding and succeeding crotchets are unaccented, and similarly with a minim.

(continued overleaf)

(v)

The keyboard accompaniment, which is simply my conflation of the vocal parts, may be used at the discretion of the choir-master, for although it seems certain that *a cappella* performance was the rule at St. Peter's, Rome, it is also certain that this was by no means typical of Renaissance practice in general.

To one distinguished writer, Curt Sachs, the technical refinement and classical poise of Palestrina's style imparts 'an austere serenity almost unique in post-medieval Christian art'; 'serene' this music certainly is, even when penitential or jubilant, but the composer's clear delight in graceful melodic shapes, sonorous and beautifully placed chords, and subtly variegated sounds achieved through vocal scoring hardly justifies the description 'austere.' On the other hand, the music reflects neither the ecstasy of Victoria nor the introspection of Lassus, but should be interpreted with a warmth of expression that reveals the delicate sensuousness of the harmony and the masterly combination of flowing lines.

DURHAM UNIVERSITY, *August* 1963   *Alec Harman*

1 Ave, Maria

Hail to thee, Mary

ADVENT

Palestrina: Ten four part motets

Palestrina: Ten four part motets

Palestrina: Ten four part motets

Palestrina: Ten four part motets

Palestrina: Ten four part motets

2 Dies sanctificatus
See now the day so blessed
CHRISTMAS

Palestrina: Ten four part motets

Palestrina: Ten four part motets

Palestrina: Ten four part motets

et lae - te - mur in e - a, ex - sul - te - mus, et lae -
and re - joice, re - joice in it, we ex - ult then, and re -

et lae - te - mur in e - a, ex - sul - te - mus, et lae -
and re - joice, re - joice in___ it, we ex - ult then, and re -

et lae - te - mur in e - a, ex - sul - te - mus, et lae -
and re - joice, re - joice in it, we ex - ult then, and re -

et lae - te - mur in e - a, ex - sul - te - mus, et lae -
and re - joice, re - joice in it, we ex - ult then, and re -

rit.

- te - mur in e - a.
- joice, re - joice in it.

- te - mur in___ e - a, ex - sul - te - mus, et lae - te - mur in e - a.
- joice, re - joice___ in it, we ex - ult then, and re - joice, re - joice in it.

- te - mur in e - a, ex - sul - te - mus, et lae - te - mur in e - a.
- joice, re - joice in it, we ex - ult then, and re - joice, re - joice in it.

- te - mur in e - a, ex - sul - te - mus, et lae - te - mur in e - a.
- joice, re - joice in it, we ex - ult then, and re - joice, re - joice in it.

3 Tribus miraculis

For these three miracles so wondrous

EPIPHANY

The Visit of the Magi, the Baptism in Jordan, and the Marriage Feast of Cana, have been regarded as typical manifestations (or epiphanies) of the Divinity of our Lord since the early days of the Church. The words "on this day" are a reminder that between the 2nd and 4th centuries, all three happenings were commemorated on Jan. 6th at various times. The Office Hymn "Hostis Herodies Impie", dating from c. 450, is a reminder of this (cf. *The English Hymnal* 38 or *A. & M. Revised* 74).

Palestrina: Ten four part motets

Palestrina: Ten four part motets

Palestrina: Ten four part motets

Palestrina: Ten four part motets

4 Ad Te levavi oculos meos*

To thee I lift mine eyes

LENT

*Part I only

Palestrina: Ten four part motets

Palestrina: Ten four part motets

Palestrina: Ten four part motets

5 Nos autem gloriari oportet

But glory now we offer

PASSIONTIDE

Palestrina: Ten four part motets

Palestrina: Ten four part motets

Palestrina: Ten four part motets

Palestrina: Ten four part motets

Palestrina: Ten four part motets

Palestrina: Ten four part motets

Palestrina: Ten four part motets

6 Haec dies quam fecit Dominus

This day is that which the Lord hath made

EASTER

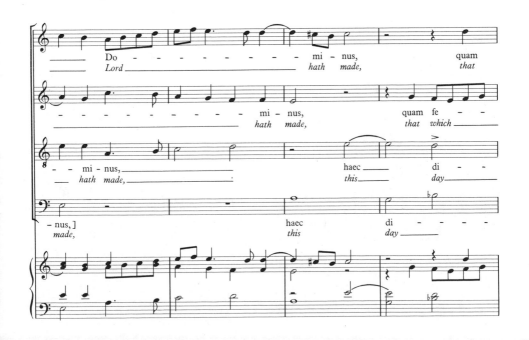

Palestrina: Ten four part motets

Palestrina: Ten four part motets

Palestrina: Ten four part motets

Palestrina: Ten four part motets

7 O Rex gloriae
King of glory thou
ASCENSION

Palestrina: Ten four part motets

Palestrina: Ten four part motets

Palestrina: Ten four part motets

Palestrina: Ten four part motets

Palestrina: Ten four part motets

Palestrina: Ten four part motets

8 Loquebantur variis Apostoli

Lo! behold in various tongues did th' Apostles speak

WHITSUN

Palestrina: Ten four part motets

Palestrina: Ten four part motets

Palestrina: Ten four part motets

Palestrina: Ten four part motets

Palestrina: Ten four part motets

Palestrina: Ten four part motets

Palestrina: Ten four part motets

9 Benedicta sit Sancta Trinitas
Ever blest be the Holy Trinity
TRINITY

Palestrina: Ten four part motets

Palestrina: Ten four part motets

Palestrina: Ten four part motets

Palestrina: Ten four part motets

Palestrina: Ten four part motets

10 Salvator mundi
O thou, world's Saviour
ALL SAINTS

Palestrina: Ten four part motets

Palestrina: Ten four part motets

Palestrina: Ten four part motets

Palestrina: Ten four part motets

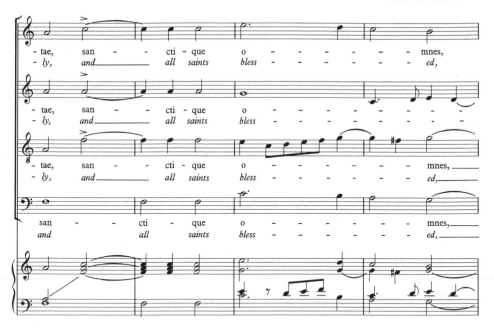

Palestrina: Ten four part motets

Palestrina: Ten four part motets

Processed and printed by
Halstan & Co. Ltd., Amersham, Bucks., England

OXFORD UNIVERSITY PRESS